www.GetKidsWriting.com

Copyright © 2020 by Get Kids Writing

This book is written by.............

About the author

_____

_____

_____

_____

_____

_____

Tips to use this book.

This isn't like a normal book- you can write and draw all over it. You can even decorate the cover.
We recommend using permanent or acryllic based pens on the cover. (Pencils don't show up well and water based pens rub off and smudge.)

Inside the book- use pens or pencils that don't soak into the paper too much so they don't show through on the other side.

Get creative and write and draw your own short stories. Let your imagination run riot!
Choose a title for each story or chapter and fill out the contents page as you go along- with your story titles or chapter.

Create a whole book of short stories or one long masterpiece. It is completely up to you.

We would love to see your creations and read your stories - please email us at info@GetKidsWriting.com or share to our Facbook page fb.com/GetKidsWriting
We will publish our favourites on our website.

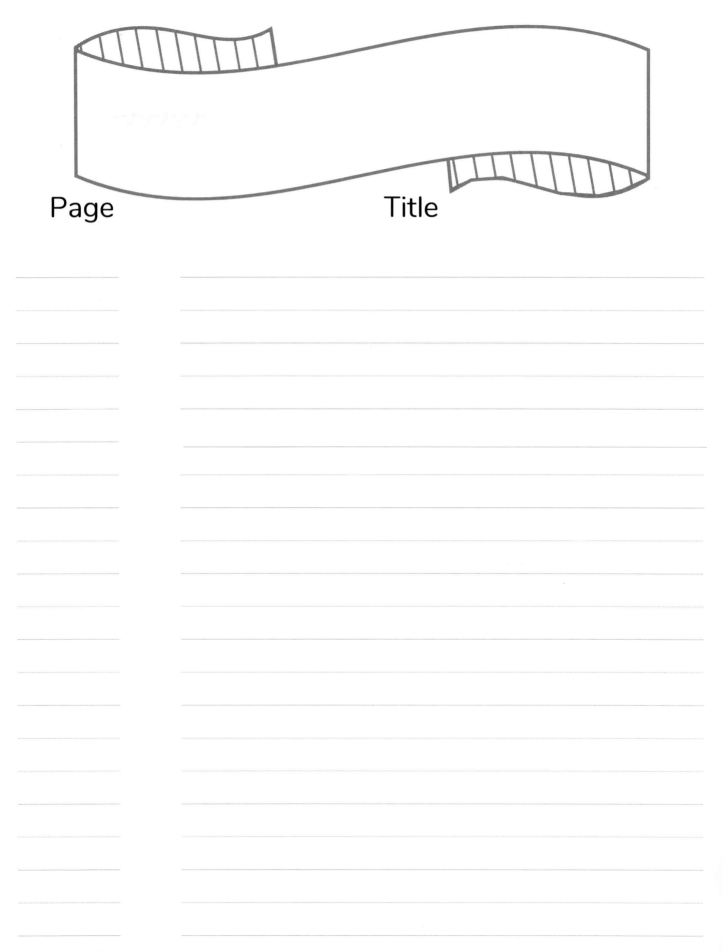

Page

Title

Use these pages to create a contents page

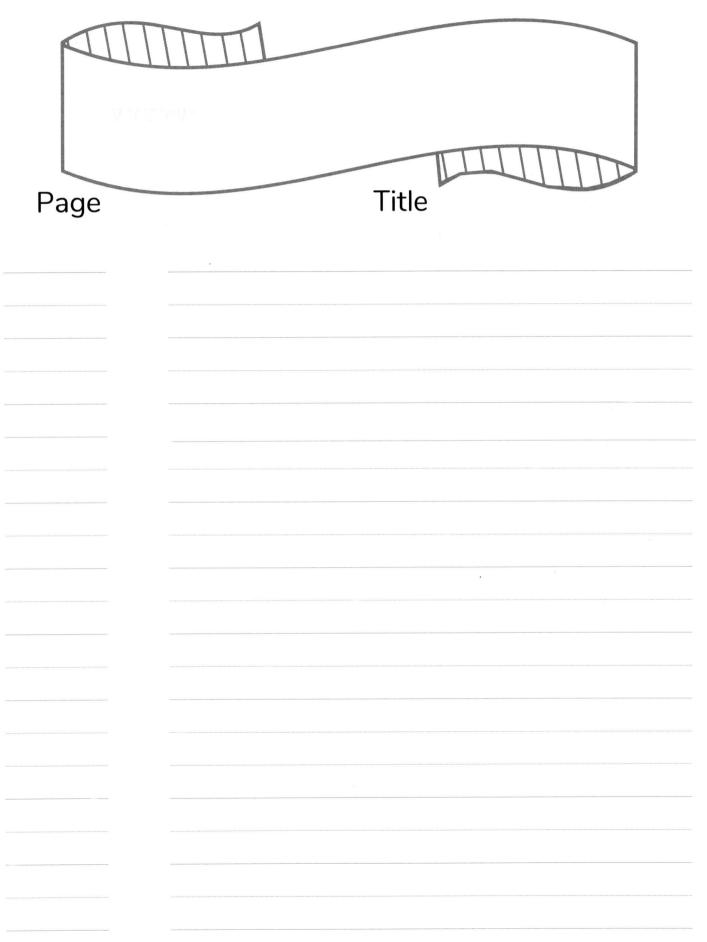

Page

Title

Use these pages to create a contents page

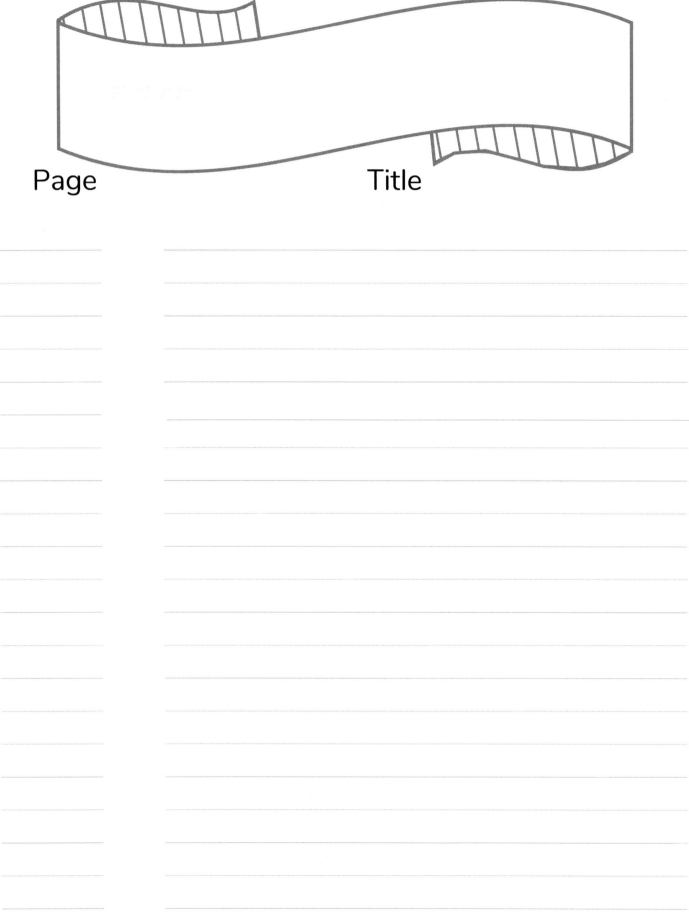

Page

Title

Use these pages to create a contents page

Made in the USA
Las Vegas, NV
17 November 2022

59594014R00046